FACE DAN(

The Rachel Farmer Trust

Rachel Farmer died on March 16th, 1993 after slipping from a steep walkway at Buoux in the south of France. A trust has been set up in her name to provide care and opportunities for the young and underprivileged. All proceeds from this book will be used in support of this charity.

A Sam & Neil Publication

ISBN 0 9522643 0 7

| S&N |
| Sam Neil |

1 9 9 3

All rights reserved. No part of this publication may be reproduced, stored in a retrieval system, or transmitted in any form or by any means, electronic, mechanical, or otherwise, without prior permission of the copyright owners.

Sam & Neil, 1 Heath Gardens, Twickenham, Middlesex, TW1 4LY.
Printed and Bound by Raithby, Lawrence and Company Ltd, Leicester.

INTRODUCTION	5
FRANCE	6
CÉÜSE	11
VERDON	17
BUOUX	23
BRITAIN	36
DERBYSHIRE	41
YORKSHIRE	51
NORTH WALES	59
INSIDE	67
RACHEL FARMER	75

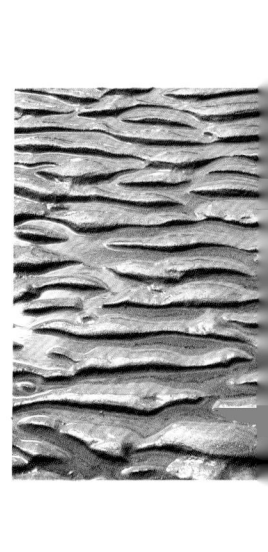

For Barry, Margaret and Suzannah.

We are a community who has lost one of its closest and most valuable members. Our lifestyle is based upon simple philosophies and desires: to experience adventure, to achieve ambitions, and to form close friendships, but above all to laugh, have fun, and get the most from life.

A small group of British climbers based in Sheffield would like to pay tribute to Rachel Farmer, a role model and friend for many, with a remarkable talent for living. The immense enthusiasm that she generated has inspired us to share a glimpse of our existence, both at home and abroad, working hard and playing hard. This book will take you on a pictorial jouney through mountains, across river gorges, and over moorlands to some of the places which briefly became her home.

'Only when you drink from the river of silence shall you indeed sing. And when you have reached the mountain top, then you shall begin to climb. And when the earth shall claim your limbs, then shall you truly dance.'

Kahlil Gibran (The Prophet)

Rachel at the **Royal Ballet School** (1980).

F R A N C E

*Bonsoir
Je m'appelle Rachel*

Le Cimai, main face.
photo: Steve Lewis

Sport climbing at **Russan**.
photo: Steve Lewis

FRANCE • 7

What is it that makes us and thousands of other dedicated sport climbers worldwide return to France, time and again? There is so much spare rock around the world just waiting to be conquered, and yet so many of our goals and dreams lie within the gorge walls of Buoux, in the cave at Volx or on top of a mountain called Céüse. The 'French magnet' is a source of mystery to many on the fringes of sport climbing, and even to those caught up in it. So often there are the crowds, the queues, the heat, and the polished holds, worn away by pilgrims, but it's just the best!

There is a strange paradox which seems inherent with the French experience. The routes are not only the world's most famous, they are show pieces in the 'laboratory' of sport climbing, where new physical and mental barriers are being discovered all the time. An ascent here can mean twice as much as one anywhere else: it is the standard, the cutting edge. The athlete comes here with hopes and expectations, prepared to do battle, but acutely aware of that ferry ticket, booked for two weeks ahead! Time is short, and not all go home victorious.

So you arrive, pure in mind and spirit, at your fighting weight ... and then the fun begins. France isn't just notorious for hard routes; the cafés, the bars, and the boulangeries will be as much your home over the next few weeks as the crags themselves. For many, those visions of hard moves become hazy before being overridden by those of croissants, glaces, bières, and the ever-pressing temptation just to sit back and look for the nearest beach.

This is the dilemma faced by the French sport-climbing devotee, and for some it can be simply overbearing. But for those who don't lose their heads and either retreat to the annals of dieting and cellars, or

photo: Steve Lewis

conversely, become completely absorbed in true holiday indulgence, there is a great prize to be won: the chance of going home a better climber, with some of the World's finest routes to your name, having experienced some of Europe's most beautiful and unspoilt heritage.

Perhaps this is the real challenge of French climbing and the secret behind its lure. It's a matter of Yin and Yang, of getting the balance right.

10 • FACE DANCING

C   É   Ü   S   E

12 • CÉÜSE

Previous page: Steve Lewis.

Climber on **Privilège du Serpent**, a classic 7c+ endurance route.
photo: Steve Lewis

CÉÜSE • 13

'**Le Cascade**'.
photo: Steve Lewis

'The World is a better place because it contains human beings who will give up ease and security in order to do what they themselves think is worth doing. They do the useless, the noble, divinely foolish and very wisest things that are done by man. And what they prove to themselves and to others is that man is no mere creature of his habits, no automaton of his routine, but that in the dust of which he is made there is also fire, lighted now and then by great winds from the sky.'

Walter Lipman (1939)

14 • CÉÜSE

The home of French stamina climbing – **Secteur Cascade**, with a climber on **Super Mickey** (7b+).
photo: Steve Lewis

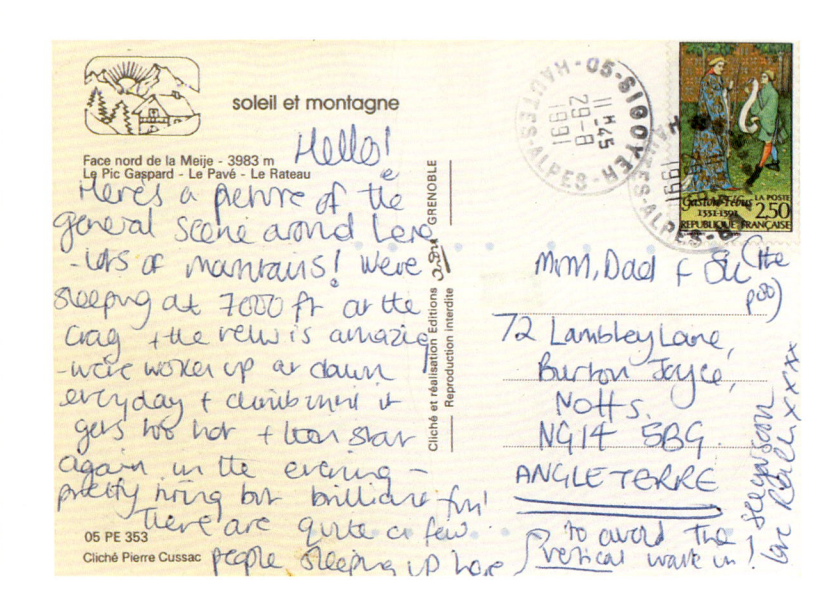

A postcard home from **Céüse**.

CÉÜSE • 15

16 • FACE DANCING

V E R D O N

'We must have a beginner's mind, free from possessing anything, a mind that knows everything is in flowing change. Nothing exists but momentarily in its present form and colour. One thing flows into another and cannot be grasped.'

Shunryu Suzuki

Rachel seconding the final pitch of **Gwendal**, (7a and 1000 ft).
photo: Neil Gresham

photo: Richie Brooks

20 • VERDON

The end of a good day.
photo: Richie Brooks

'What we get from this adventure is just sheer joy, and joy is after all the end of life. We eat and make money to be able to enjoy life. This is what life means and what it is for.'

George Mallory

22 • FACE DANCING

B U O U X

24 • BUOUX

'But you, children of space, you restless in rest, you shall not be trapped nor tamed. Your house shall not be an anchor but a mast ... For that which is boundless in you abides in the mansion of the sky, whose door is the morning mist, and whose windows are the songs and silences of the night.'

Kahlil Gibran, (The Prophet)

Previous page: Richie Brooks

Practice makes perfect. Ian Harrison working the moves of **Territoire de Fièvre** (7c+), on the West Face.
photo: Steve Lewis

Life on **La Plage**.
photo: Steve Lewis

26 • BUOUX

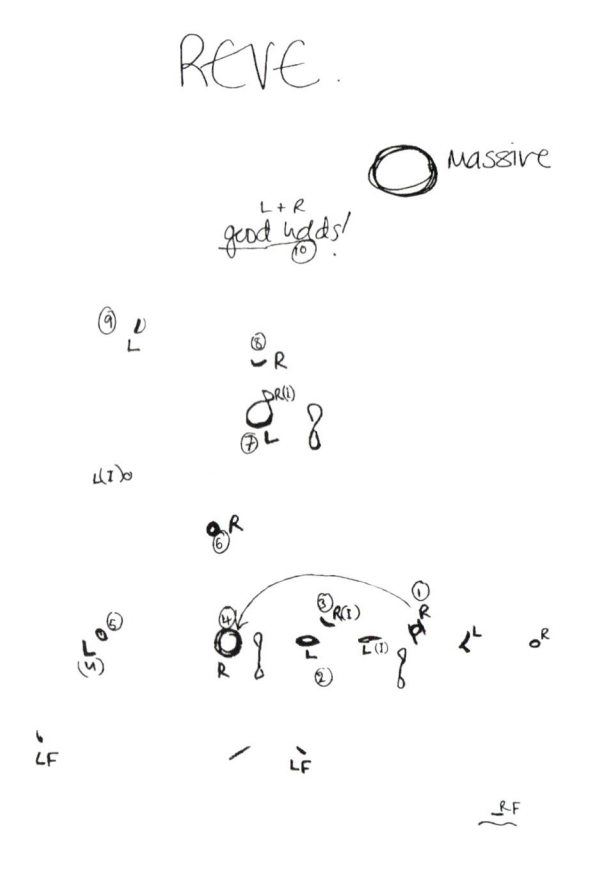

Rachel climbing
in **Secteur Derive**.
photo: Neil Gresham

Rachel's sequence map of '**Réve**'.

Neil Gresham on
Réve d'un Papillon (8a).
photos: Sam Grimmer

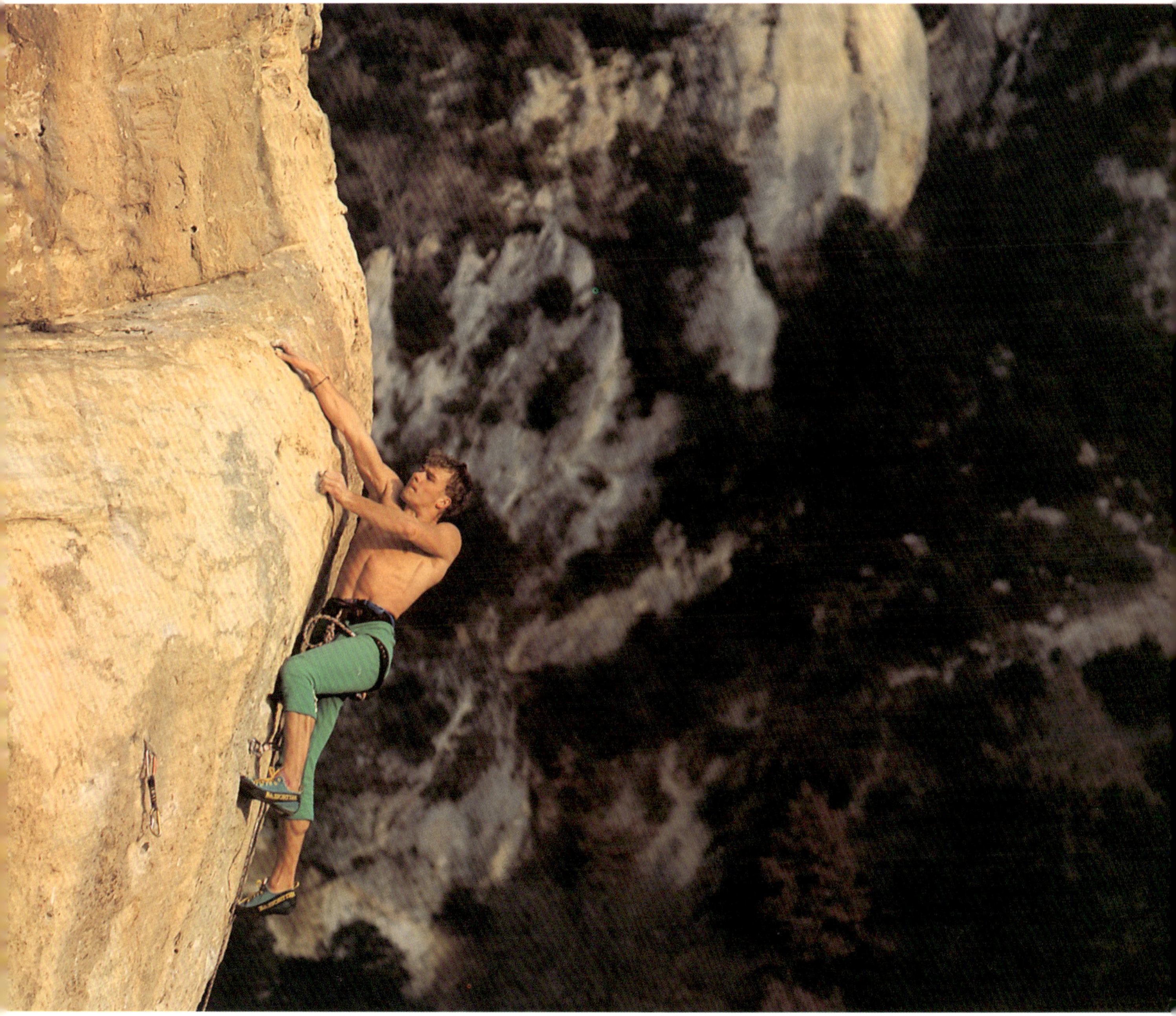

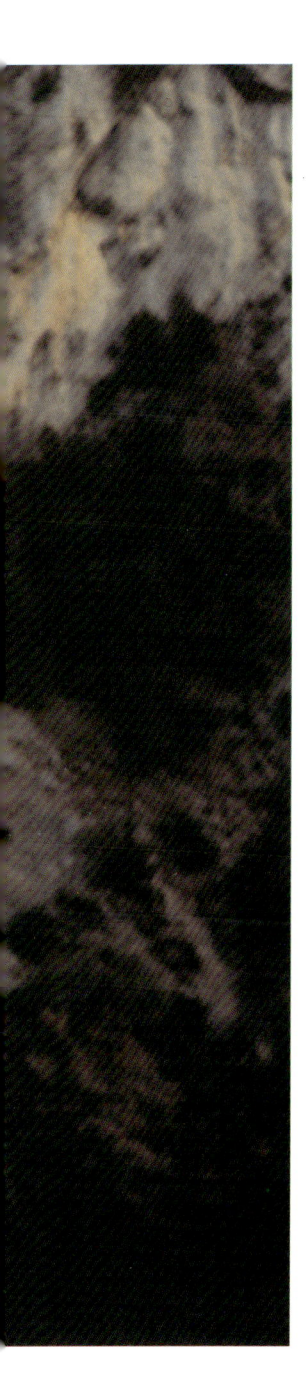

'Passion creates possibility'

Chris Walmsley 'topping out'
on **Exces de Zéle** (7c+).
photo: Steve Lewis

Ian Harrison cuts loose on **Exces de Zéle** (7c+).
photo: Steve Lewis

BUOUX • 31

A postcard from Ben Moon, sent home to the Sheffield crew after repeating **Chouca** in 1985. At the time this was the World's hardest climb, and it is now probably the most famous and notorious of all French sport routes.

Rachel working the hardest moves of **Chouca** (8a+) in 1992.
photo: Neil Trimboy

'Difficulties are just problems to overcome afterall.'

Shackleton

The crux sequence of **Chouca** (8a+).
photos: Neil Trimboy

BUOUX • 33

34 • FACE DANCING

"To laugh is to risk appearing the fool, to weep is to risk appearing sentimental, to reach out for another is to risk exposing your true self. To place your ideas, your dreams before the crowd is to risk their loss, to love is to risk not being loved in return, to live is to risk dying , to hope is to risk despair. To try is to risk failure, but the risk must be taken, because the greatest hazard in life is to risk nothing. The person who risks nothing, does nothing, is nothing. He may avoid suffering, but he simply cannot learn, feel, change, grow, love, live. Chained by his certitudes, he is a slave. He has forfeited freedom. Only a person who risks is free."

Unknown

36 • BRITAIN

BRITAIN

'We are the seeds of the tenacious plant, and it is in our ripeness and our fullness that we are given to the wind and scattered.'

Kahlil Gibran (The Prophet)

Gritstone moors in the dark Peak.
photo: Richie Brooks

There is perhaps no other climbing area worldwide to surpass the United Kingdom for offering such geological diversity within such a small area. Each cragging excursion becomes its own individual adventure, so different from the previous, provided of course, that you manage to resist the temptation purely to frequent your local cliff.

A unique code of 'crag-specific' ethics seems to have evolved in an attempt to preserve the character of each area; whether it is the breathtaking scale and sense of adventure of the Welsh mountain crags or the stark contrast of the 'weird and wonderful' slate quarries just down the way. In Yorkshire and the Peak District, the powerful and gymnastic, bolted limestone crags provide a harmonious contrast to the neighbouring gritstone edges, which remain the mental domain of balance and technique. Surely there is something here for everyone.

Our climbing lacks bland consistency, and, although the British are held as old-fashioned and eccentric by some of the world's top climbing nations, it could be argued that our ethics show a heightened understanding of the true values at the routes of our sport. Rather than prisoners of our self-imposed rules, we have attempted to progress in symbiosis with nature, rising to meet its standard rather than bolting or chiselling it down to ours. Inconsistent though we may be, our sea-cliff crags remain as sinister or as safe as the wind and waves have designed them to be; from the immaculate, fractured Pembrokeshire limestone with abundant natural protection, to soul-searching runouts on dramatic but dubious Gogarth shale. At the same time we are not afraid to move with the times, as the emergence of the Great Orme as the new 'European-style' coastal venue for British sport climbing has proved.

However, the British Utopia – though romantic – is far from stable. As with the global environment, there will always be the conflict between the squanderers, hungry for short-term success, and those who are determined to save our non-renewable climbing resources for the future.

And all this fuss over such a seemingly insignificant and tiny area. The untrained eye would dismiss most of these places as 'small game' compared to the great walls of Yosemite or the Verdon, and those who do grow to love them may be quickly disheartened by the ever-disappointing weather. Yet these crags are our heritage, and the UK has produced some of the world's finest climbers, their successes having been fuelled more by passion than perfect facilities. Since Haskett-Smith's ascent of Napes Needle in 1886 up to Moon's ascent of Hubble in 1990, the British have been out there through heatwaves and snowstorms, from limestone to gritstone, doing what they do. Very well.

photo: Graham Hulm

40 • FACE DANCING

DERBYSHIRE

42 • DERBYSHIRE

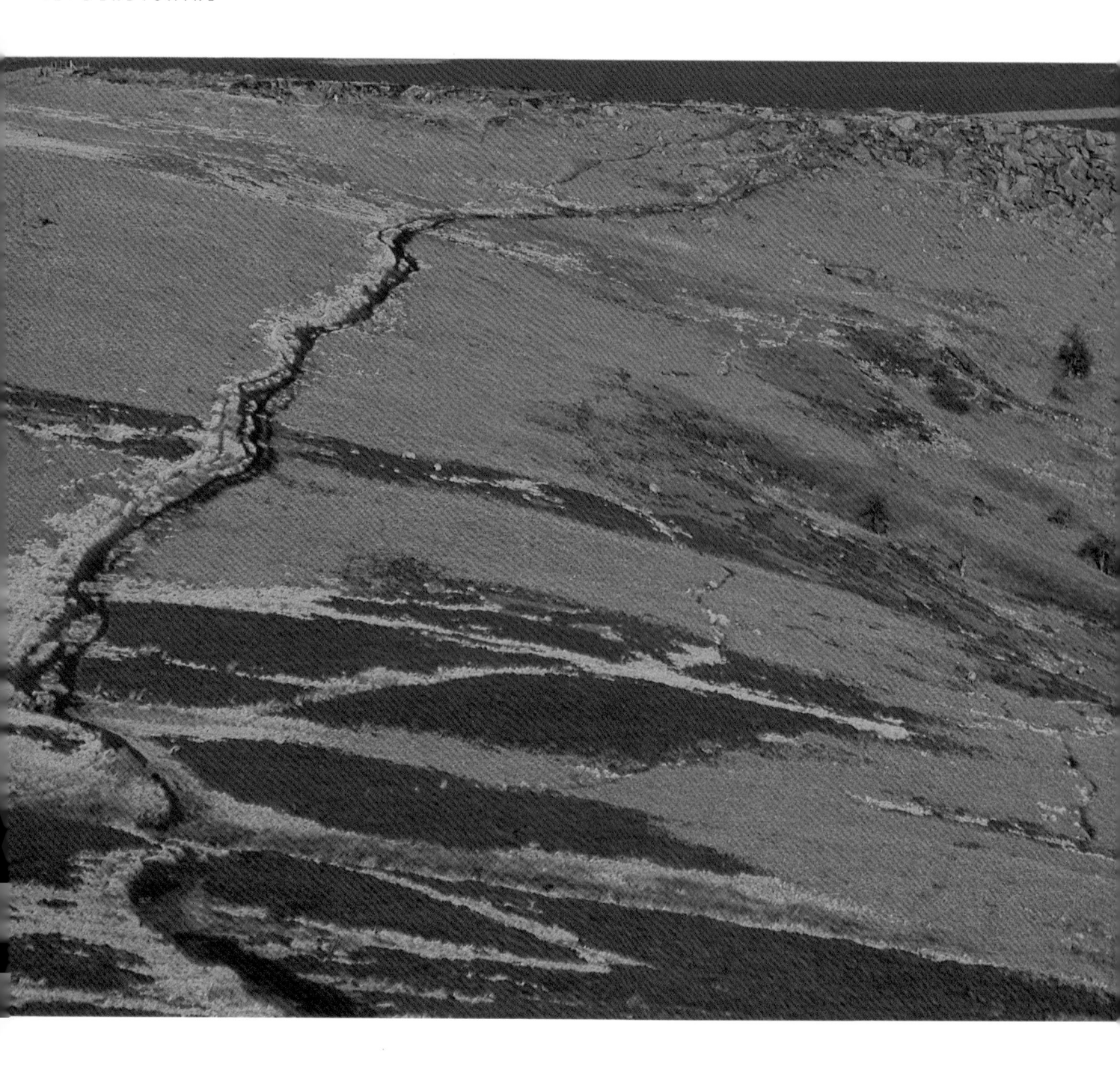

'It is not growing like a tree
In bulk, doth make men better be;
Or standing long an oak, three hundred year,
To fall a log at last, dry, bald and sere:
A lily of a day
Is fairer far in May,
Although it fall and die that night;
It was the plant and flower of light.
In small proportions we just beauties see;
And in short measures, life may perfect be.'

Ben Jonson

Previous page: Richie Brooks

Burbage in Autumn.
photo: Richie Brooks

Rachel and friends bouldering at
Joe's Playground on **Froggatt Edge**.
photo: Laura Meegan

Stanage moors.
photo: Richie Brooks

'To see, it is not enough to open the eyes.
One must above all open one's heart.'

Gaston Rebuffat (1959)

Neil Gresham on
London Wall (E5 6a),
at **Millstone Edge**.
photo: Sam Grimmer

46 • DERBYSHIRE

'Now understand me well – it is provided in the essence of things, that from any fruition of success, no matter what, shall come forth something to make a greater struggle necessary.'

Walt Whitman

Rachel working and redpointing **Let the Tribe Increase** on **Rubicon Wall** in the White Peak. This was the first 7c+ to be climbed by a British woman and the ascent was made in only two days. Routes such as this one epitomise limestone climbing in the Peak District, where the difficulty of each movement more than compensates for the lack of height of the crag. photos: Graham Hulm

Rubicon Wall
in Watercumjolly.
photo: Richie Brooks

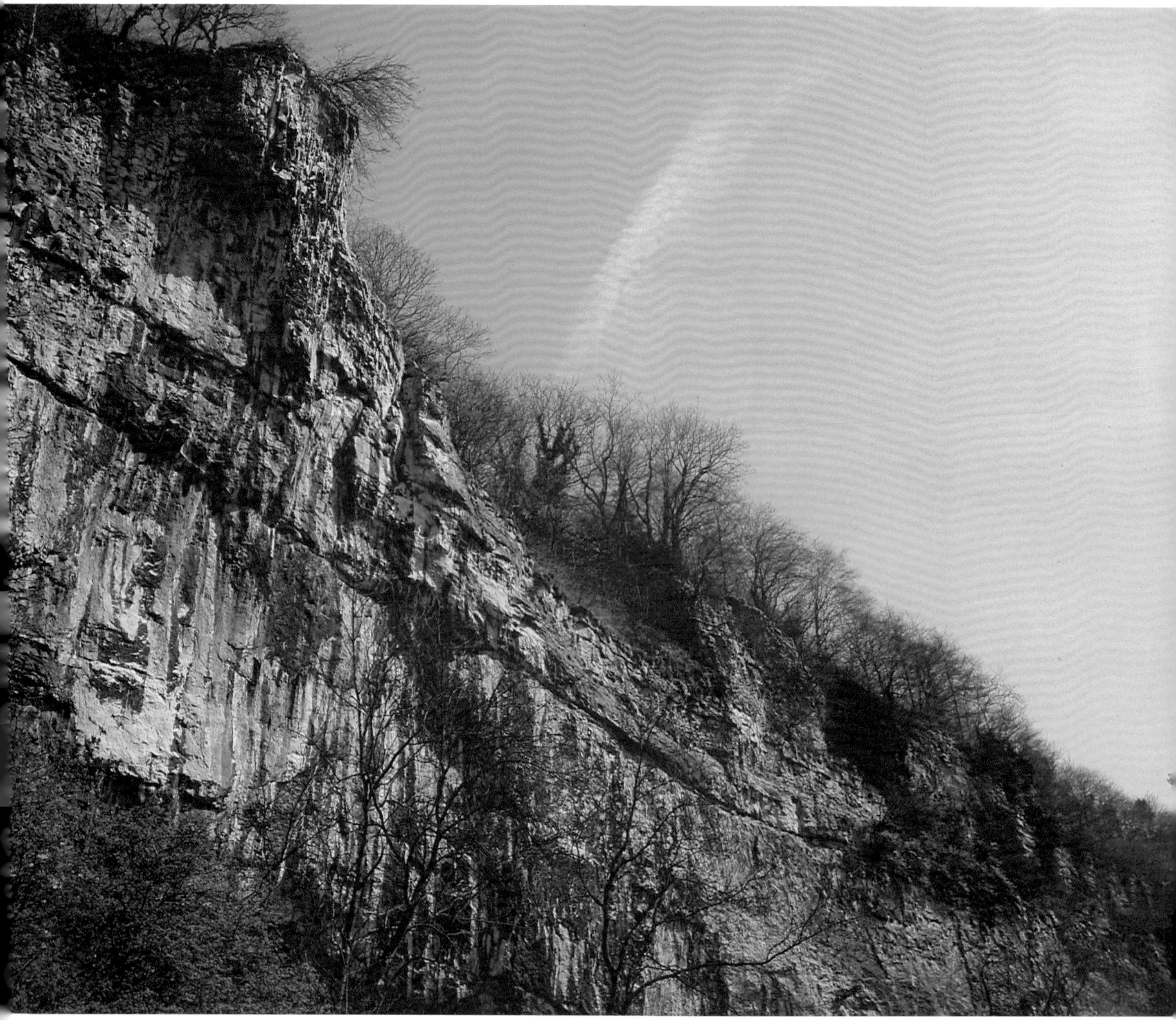

Saturday June 15

> Raventor
> Old Sardine (4 falls)
> Indecent (2 falls).
>
> Pm. minor ops (H1)
> - saw ① Vasectomy
> ② Cyst removed from breast
> ③ toenails removed.

Rachel's diary (June 1991)

Gavin Ellis spots John Welford on **Power Band**, a boulder traverse at **Raventor**.
photo: Richie Brooks

Raventor in Millersdale, a venue that has been synonymous with the evolution of British sport climbing.
photo: Richie Brooks

50 • FACE DANCING

YORKSHIRE

52 • YORKSHIRE

Previous page:
Climber on **L'Obsession**
(7c+) at **Malham Cove**.
photo: Richie Brooks

'If we stick at it we'll get there. Women peak late. I put my money on Rachel. She has such good physique and a "go-for-it" attitude. She'll be the first British woman to climb the French 8a.'

Delyth Goodey (**High** Magazine, October 1992)

Malham Cove, the centrepiece of Yorkshire climbing.
photo: Neil Gresham

Rachel working on **Le Maximum** (7c+) and opposite, the crux move.
photos: Noel Thom

Rachel Farmer on **Raindogs** (8a/E7 6b).
photos: Noel Thom

Rachel's diary (September 1992)

'RACHEL TICKS RAINDOGS!

'Rachel Farmer took 7 days to become the first British woman to climb the coveted grade of 8a. Of the route Raindogs at Malham she says, 'I think this was a fairly suitable route for me, being a power-endurance route with no hard moves, but at the same time no shake outs, you have to keep moving on it!' Although she got the final hold of the route on the end of her fourth day, she decided to leave it over the summer as it became greasy and impossible to climb.'

OTE Magazine (NO.32)

'As is often the case, the successful ascent had come when least expected after all expectation and hope had seemingly evaporated. Sport climbing in which defeat is often unintentionally self imposed often seems to run like that. The day was almost done, everyone else had packed up, when Rachel set off up the route simply to strip the route of the quickdraws; moments later she found herself at the belay. Rachel confided that all day she had been feeling undue pressures, not least from sponsoring manufacturers. Had her success on Raindogs, I wondered, brought with it for Rachel unlooked-for demands and expectations? But no, she appears to remain blithely unaffected by such considerations, her primary ambition is still to experience and enjoy as much climbing as possible and not a desperate desire simply to go one better as soon as possible.'

HIGH Magazine (Nov 1992)

56 • YORKSHIRE

'The light that burns twice as bright burns half as long, and you have burned so very brightly ... '

'Dr Tyrell' (Blade Runner)

Rachel working on **Comedy** (7c) at **Kilnsey**.
photo: Neil Gresham

58 • FACE DANCING

NORTH WALES

'"Hot soup was a jolly good idea, it's so cold this morning but then it's very early, the sun is only just coming up – look!" They finished their breakfast watching the blue water turn to dancing gold, even the rocks gleamed in the sun.'

Enid Blyton (The Adventurous Four)

Llyn Llydaw, Snowdon
photo: Richie Brooks

Previous page: **Snowdon**
:Richie Brooks

Sun beam in the
Ogwen Valley
photo: Graham Hulm

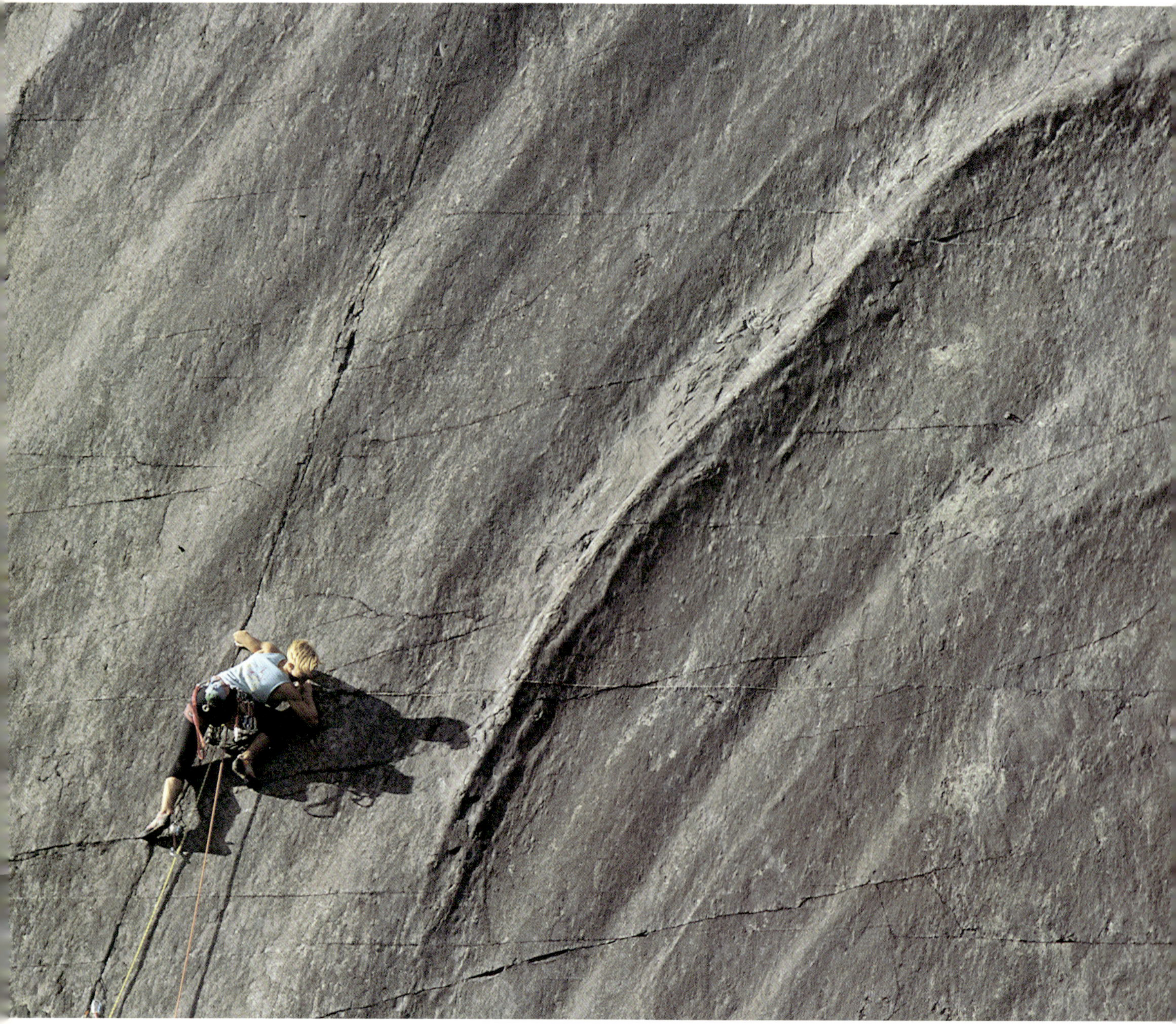

'Better to be a tiger for a day than a sheep for a lifetime.'

Inscription on memorial
plaque for **Alex Macintyre**.
(Killed in the Himalaya, 1982)

Neil Gresham on **Rainbow of recalcitrance**
(E6 6b), in the **Dinorwig** slate quarries.
photo: Graham Hulm

64 • NORTH WALES

Adam Wainwright on the first
ascent of **Melancholie** (8b),
at **Lower Pen Trwyn**.
photo: Richie Brooks

Lower Pen Trwyn; sun, sea, and bolts in
North Wales – with Mark Leach climbing
the classic 8a, **Statement of Youth**.
photo: Richie Brooks

NORTH WALES • 65

66 • FACE DANCING

I N S I D E

68 • INSIDE

*Came 17th overall
— massive roof ! nightmare
I need strong arms !* Sunday 20

Previous page: **Sheffield**.
photo: Richie Brooks

Birmingham (1991).
photo: Ian Smith

*Laval — wrong sequence
+ inability to hang
there to work it out when
holds are very greasy
+ hot !
Try + climb :
quickly between good
holds but learn
to hang on holds every
2-3 moves + LOOK
at the next
few holds.
Don't get a sequence +
stick to it
— keep options open.*

Birmingham (1992).
photo: Dod Miller

Rachel's diary extracts from World Cup competitions at Frankfurt and Laval.

Rachel competing at **Birmingham** (1992). 15th overall and the highest placed British Woman.
photo: Peter Brooks

Rachel flashing the women's final route at the British Open (1992), held at the **Foundry** in **Sheffield**.
photo: John Houlihan

'4.30 pm, Sunday 4th October. Superfinal.

'The audience is buzzing, we have waited over an hour watching the route setters tweak the superfinal routes. Building these routes must be a nightmare, they have to be hard enough to split the best climbers, with, ideally, only the very best climber topping out. We wait to see if they have done a good job. The women's superfinal takes a steep direct line up a 30-degree overhanging pillar and headwall above, its angle should suit the more powerful Rachel Farmer, who climbs first. Rachel climbs positively and quickly; positive snatches up the pillar take her onto the headwall, where suddenly, she pauses, crabs her feet, stretches for an undercut and falls. She must be disappointed but she also smiles, in truth I think she's just glad to get it over with; at least the route setters are relieved. In contrast Felicity (Butler) climbs slowly, she wobbles so much low down that I'm sure she will fall, however what she lacks in power she makes up for in stamina and technique. The leaning pillar is a controlled fight, but somehow she reaches Rachel's high point, then (oh so easily) she pulls on the undercut and the audience ignites. Felicity knows she has won, but climbs to the top anyway. Her reign is safe, at least until next week when the two meet again in Tokyo … It's a shared group high that surpasses even Leeds '89. Now all that remains is to party, Fat Cat, Madras, Broadfield, but that's a different and perhaps more entertaining story.'

Dave Pegg (**High** Magazine, November 1992)

Bouldering at the **Foundry**
photo: Simon Scully

72 • INSIDE

Anxious moments at
the British Open (1992).
photo: John Houlihan

bouldering comp in cellar. brilliant laugh. everyone came round. Nick (sellars) won.

Rachel's diary (January 1993)

Training underground in **Sheffield**. The new cult 'cellar' scene typifies the modern British sport climber – with a low budget but high levels of motivation.
photo: Sam Grimmer

INSIDE • 73

74 • FACE DANCING

RACHEL FARMER

Rachel Kathryn Farmer was born on January 27th, 1970, in Bakersfield, Nottingham, where she also attended primary school. Her early passion for dance was developed at Miss Morrison's school in Nottingham and she went on to train at the Royal Ballet School in Richmond Park. After three years at White Lodge she sustained a tendon injury and decided to switch careers. Rachel returned to Burton Joyce in Nottingham to attend Carlton-le-Willows Secondary School and then went on to study Medicine at Sheffield University. This began after an intensive 'year out' in which she studied for an additional A level while teaching aerobics, and working at a restaurant, a nightclub, and a rehabilitation centre! She also took time to travel to Europe, America, and Egypt before starting university, although it was not until she commenced her medical studies that she discovered climbing in the neighbouring Peak District.

In her three-year association with rock climbing, Rachel Farmer showed more rapid progress than almost anyone in the history of the sport. From novice level in 1990, by 1993 she became the first British woman to climb the highly acclaimed grade of French '8a' while at the same time competing for Britain in the World Series, in which she was ranked 15th.

"Sometimes ruthless determination is associated with achievement at the top level of the sport. Despite being thrown in at the highest levels, Rachel did not lose touch with the basic enjoyment and excitement which started her climbing."

Roger Payne (National officer for the **BMC**)

'She offered women around her a role model they could more easily identify with than the superstars of the US or Continent.'

Mountain Review (May 1993)

Previous page: Rachel Farmer (Winter 1973)

"Rachel never seemed competitive in any way; she was motivated more by inner strengths and personal goals."

Ruth Jenkins & Anne Arran (**High** Magazine, May 1993)

"Although she was a shining example to other women, she could certainly hold her own with the boys, and her accomplishments will long stand as an inspiration to everyone … She was at times shy, often self-doubting, sometimes infuriatingly indecisive, and yet it was her exuberant effervescent nature which always came to the fore with an enthusiasm that was impossible to ignore … Her passion for life took some fuelling, and her seemingly never-ending appetite was legendary."

Hamish Morrison (Friend and climbing companion)

"She could often be seen dancing away at Kiki's nightclub, once even with her leg in plaster! Nothing could keep her inactive; she had the energy of ten normal people! She showed us all how to take ourselves a bit less seriously, have some sources of interest apart from medicine, but still get the work done."

Lea Forsyth (Fellow medical student)

"Rachel was a communicator."

Chris Welsh (Dean of the Faculty of Medicine, **Sheffield University**)

"I believe her philosophies were to spread cheerfulness, fun, and love around; to move on to new things whilst holding on to the most important parts of your past; to develop your own potential by setting your own goals and striving to achieve them; to live life to the full as much as possible, and communicate and share that enjoyment with others."

Margaret Farmer (Rachel's Mother)

Extracts from Rachel's memorial service held at the **Foundry**, **Sheffield** (April 28th 1993)

Neil Gresham: (Conception and Editorial)

Sam Grimmer: (Design and Art Direction)

Sam and Neil would like to express their sincere thanks to the following for their invaluable help during the production of this book:

Murray Clayton (for the title). Simon Kincaid, Joanne Smith and Paul Deegan (Quotations). Stephanie "The Boss" Jackson and Liz "The Whizz" Wheeler (editorial assistance). Jonathan "Biffa" Bacon (Macintosh consultancy). Lynne Brown (production advice). Mathew Gould at Raithby Lawrence (printing liaison). "Smythe" (player). Karen Russel (maid). Gill Kent at On The Edge Magazine, Ian Smith at High Magazine, Tom Prentice at Climber Magazine, Mary Comber at Health & Fitness Magazine, and The Dancing Times (publicity). Phil and Julian at The Foundry (launch support). Thanks most of all to; Charlie Barwell and Tony Ingham at Cotswold, Jamie Cameron at Snow & Rock, Gordon Fraser at Ventura, Andy Bowman at Eclipse, Mark Vallance at Wild Country, Fred Smith at High Places, Ian "Squawk" Dunne at Bendcrete and Graham "Streaky" Desroy at DR, without whose generosity this project would never have got off the drawing board.

Photography, (and previously uncredited pictures):

Richie Brooks (+ pages: 8, 10, 18, 21, 22, 34, 38, 43, 58, 63, 64, 65).
Steve Lewis (+ pages: 9, 13, 14, 16, 29).
Neil Gresham (+ pages: 8, 76, 77, 80).
Noel Thom.
Graham "Mungo" **Hulm** (+ pages: 3, 63).
Sam Grimmer.
Mike "the Milkman" **Rodrigue** (+ pages: 38, 44, 56).
Ian Smith (+ pages: 72, 74).
Neil Trimboy.
John Houlihan.
Hamish Morrison (+ pages: 38, 50).
Peter Brooks.
Simon Scully.
Heinz Zak (+ pages: 35, 40).
Barry Farmer (+ pages: 5, 75, 76, 77).

Richie Brooks
(Principal photography)

Steve Lewis
(Principal photography)

The Rachel Farmer Trust gratefully acknowledge:

WILD COUNTRY

BOREAL (Eclipse)

ASOLO (Ventura)

EDELWEISS (High Places)

BENDCRETE Climbing Walls

DR Climbing Walls

COTSWOLD The Outdoor People

SNOW & ROCK

OUTSIDE

THE FOUNDRY

80 • FACE DANCING

R K F

'This is the place that I loved her,
and these are the friends that she had.
Long may the mountain ring,
to the sound of her laughter ...'

Neil Finn (from She Goes On)